Lived in Bars

Lived in Bars

poems by
Erica Hoffmeister

STUBBORN MULE PRESS
DEVIL'S ELBOW, MO

Stubborn Mule Press
Devil's Elbow, MO
stubbornmulepress.com

All poems copyright © Erica Hoffmeister, 2019
zhoffmeister@gmail.com

First Edition 11 7 5 3 2 1
ISBN: 978-1-950380-36-7
LCCN: 2019942220
Design, edits and layout: Jeanette Powers
stubbornmulepress@gmail.com @stubbornmulepress
CoverArt: Jon Lee Grafton
Interior & Bio Photos: Erica Hoffmeister

Are you really reading this? Congratulations, we love you. No one but the author can really claim rights to their work, no matter what law says what. And we can't really do anything about theft, whatever that means, so here is our pact: Be cool, be kind, don't steal, email the author if you like or want to riff off their work. Also, let us at Stubborn Mule know if you want to write a review, we'll share it and your review publication, too. Go ahead and use passages for reviews, accolades, or epigraphs, give credit where credit is due. Let's stay radical, share with us our honor among anarchists.

*Thank you to everyone and everything
I've ever found home in, if only
for a brief moment.*

And to The Road, my mistress.

Table of Contents

World's End	9
Hemet, California	10
Bar Graffiti	12
The Mission Inn	14
Diabla	17
Pacific Coast	18
Delirium	20
The Rainbow Bar	22
In the Need For Gas Money	23
Carnivorous Sky	24
Snook's Bottom	25
Phantom Limb	27
I Know I Shouldn't	29
Ten Dozen Breweries	30
Linger	31
The Overlook Hotel	32
South of Stateline	33
Rattlesnake	35
Waxahachie	36
Southwestern	37
San Antonio	38
Souvenir	39
The Wild One	40
The Bum Steer	42
Pops	44
The Salton Sea	45
The Ocean and the I-10	46

Dirty	48
It Could Be Anywhere	49
In the Deep South	50
Panama City Beach	51
Sand / Cement / Gravel / Water	52
Key West	54
Tampa	55
Charleston, South Carolina	56
Jack of the Wood	57
Record Store Day	58
The Center of the World	59
New Jersey	60
Americana	62
Ohio	63
Lou Ella	64
It's Jazz Night	65
70-W	66
Off Highway 55	68
Dakota Landlock	69
Tennessee	71
The One and Only	72
Zion	73
Space Between	74
Man-Made	75
Nomad	76
Zephyr	77
De Novo	78

WORLD'S END

flat-earth drunk. I left my convictions with Jesus Christ
on a train the day my father died. I had just turned 30.
It was supposed to be Paris. I felt as the exact temperature
of tepid coffee. An indescribable disappointment.
I was supposed
to see the world
turn. Somewhere in the distant past, an ex-husband is praying
for my after-
life.

HEMET, CALIFORNIA

is not where I'm from. But it's where I began.

In Vegas, a neon graveyard hums past lives, burned out bulbs,
bright lights. Burned out
bright—

this is how you found me.

Primitive. Known as a "strong one," I was born
in a blizzard— a white
out. Not that dirt hilltop, not that catholic hospital
with the nuns for midwives, but
somewhere
it was snowing hard. After all,

a blizzard is always raging *somewhere*, and to avoid one
altogether is sheer luck. Like becoming pregnant. Fat.
You know, just sitting around and waiting for something—
something big to happen.

With bruised tailbones, I left a lover in the desert to die,
bones discarded in my backseat, human flesh consumed
by coyotes, circling—
I held the match the day the Santa Ana's ripped my
childhood home into two parts:
before and after.

"House-fire" means something different to different people.
To me, it was the same day
my best friend's uncle died. We blew bubbles on the side of
the road when my car's tires stopped rotating forward, the day
we realized we weren't in control of anything. No
one ever was.

After that house was rebuilt, we dug a pit and threw our
childhood in it. Lit the surviving *things*

into flames. There was nothing left to save
once an eviction notice was nailed to the front door, anyway.
I had nothing left
to run to,
but an address I've kept on my driver's license ever since.

Firestorms
blown out like birthday candles, tiny wax moments
I used to share with
my father. We were born almost exactly
twenty years apart: that melting
German chocolate icing, melting into
two different people who'd never speak
to each other again. Dripping down the sides
of boxed cake, Oh! Those nutritious '90s, our hands
made of chocolate as we ate it in pieces in a photo of an event
I honestly don't remember. With a man I don't remember.
Somewhere

in San Bernardino,
Hemet, Riverside County,
Joshua Tree. Los
Angeles, San
Diego. Everywhere
in between.

I read the person that asks where
I'm from and a city falls out of my mouth. As if I'm
ashamed of all the places I've made my bones.
The years wept for a dead animal
mounted above a charred fireplace.

This is who I am:
Rotted, melted, aflame
in the California desert. Not where
I began,
but where I've always
ended.

33.72682, -116.94529

BAR GRAFFITI

on bathroom stalls scratched and scribbled over layers of time, erased and painted over again in a matrix of love notes, confessions, advice. Authors, nameless. Shamelessly etched for a temporary moment in a smoke cloud whim-spit of rebellion:

The Cherry Bomb
>   *I'm in love with*
>   *you*
>   *and I don't*
>   *want to be*
>   *anymore*

sprawled diagonal across etched wood in tiny lettering, the bottom corner reserved for tear-stained stilettos on a Saturday night at the dirtiest dive this side of North County line, where the salty air tastes like Mexican tap water

>   *I'M IN LOVE WITH A FANTASY*

written in bold red marker, all caps, but you think— aren't we all?

>   *Kill your parents*

and

>   *Smash your TV*

precariously parallel in opposing positions, offering only these two options to follow an identity crisis just a quarter century into this vapid life; or perhaps it elicits a sense of adventure once covered by the two inch patch of black sharpie marker creatively omitting the bridge that kept us together—

>   *He was happy before*
>   *we met*

drew me closer to the door handle. A talisman, a time-shifting vortex

> Z *This way to the ministry!* Z

> FUCK TRUMP

stitched above the toilet, a societal swirl of childhood and adulthood, worlds melting together like frozen yogurt from Dairy Queen, chocolate-sprinkled dipped cones my dad used to buy me before airshows. Complexities intertwined between conflicting ideals fated to meet one another. Dandelion roars. Agoraphobic. Homeless.

> *Slut*
> *bitch*
> *For a good time call...*

The worst of us all, scribbled out. Sketches of the human spectrum in our most private moments

I: all of these moments Sorrow hung softly above the stall. I watched each one of them pass in and out, dig through pockets and purses for some way to leave a mark, a remembrance

I: a dull pocketknife, simply carving a line around the edges, a canyon arrow pointing me elsewhere

32.728771, -117.163538

THE MISSION INN

Birthplace, birthmarks, scars across the left cheek ripped wide in 1989: there's a place I rarely consider home, tucked neatly in the middle of other places that matter more (sometimes).

We'd go to The Spaghetti Factory every year for my birthday. I'd order spumoni: this is an example of failed memory. When I was 16, my Grandfather Fritz died of lung cancer. The last day my family visited him before he died, I went to Disneyland instead with my then boyfriend, the one I dated to act much older than my age, to skip all the steps of adolescence that seemed difficult and trite. I'll harbor this decision in my gut for my life thereafter. Like a sunken ship, waterlogged wood held together by violent currents; Ursula impaled with a splintered mast. Fritz and his wife owned a brick house, a masonry business with our surname hand-painted on buildings and work trucks. My whole damn childhood smelled like brick and mortar. That whole damn town does.

They've named Magnolia Street so because it is lined with Magnolia trees. Thick, soft petals sprinkled along sidewalks. Dish soap fragrance, equivalent taste. Somewhat similar to the vodka in my grandmother's coffee. The matriarch who lived in an apartment building across from the park where the grass was made up entirely of those palm-sized, silken Magnolia petals. I don't remember her much sober, before she went blind from a stroke. Six decades of vodka coffees and Virginia Slims: another false memory, like Jenga blocks stacked to be knocked down.

When we moved to the desert, I missed how dew formed on the orange blossoms, lit up the sky with their sweet aroma. How big the world felt before. How streets and names and places haunted me with tastes and smells. I'd visit that birth-town as an adult and cry into my Dairy Queen ice cream cone— one of the last few walk-up Dairy Queens in the country, refusing to be bought out and sold for disappointing burgers and the terrible choice to get rid of chocolate sprinkles. Because that was only topping I'd ever choose: when I'd barely reach my dad's knees in height, side-by-side with his matching chocolate-sprinkled cone, when he still thought of me and our likeness fondly. I'd haunt all those places myself, it all tasting like a Molotov cocktail of childhood scents. Nostalgia-sick from birth. I'll chase the high of this longing forever.

Here, in the center of it all, stands the grand Mission Inn. Tonight is different than my past visits: Christmas lights as a kid / a honeymoon suite, once. Twenty-five years after we left a cardboard box rental on the wrong side of the tracks, I'm dressed as my mother in a neon purple Prince t-shirt and Joan Jett leather jacket wandering between past lives. Crimped with Aqua Net hair like a beauty queen in the need for a strong drink. There are club beats pumping through the thighs of college girls outside and me in the back of the bar downstairs listening to a woman sing Etta James in finger waves. Her voice is as silky as the deep slit down her red dress, curves sweltering in mixed worlds. Everyone I know is bouncing in back patio warm-light; I'm on a back barstool darkened under whisky on rocks.

There's an old man sitting in a polite corner. He wears the camouflaged scent of a nursing home— rubber tint, sharp syringe, skin saddened from memory. It must be strange to see a girl, young in pink fluorescent lip gloss, hiding between orders of blended scotch in an attempt to resurrect the dead. He shares a smile with me, an hour of time. Revisits daylight savings and how his War turned back the spring hour with napalm, how he lost legs in a decade of hope forgotten between palm trees and revolution. He shares a common drink and a common song, discusses ink etched into my own skin, skin revived with a long love of freedom he wished still lingered on locks he cut off generations ago.

It was a cool reminder:

this whole place, where the orange groves used to blow through the Santa Ana's. A small fraction of commonality. Connected. Two people from opposite spectrums of human existence laced with their own memories of this place. Pieced together in a mosaic of music, time evaporated, two breaths of past lives exhaled in unison.

33.983373, -117.373004

DIABLA

Fire-breathing, flame-storming, desert-chasing, long-winded woman. The kind that stops your heart from beating. One hand on the wheel, the other out an open window, grasping tufts of memory, grains of sand falling between fingers.

Time, wraithlike: a past that lingers just beyond a bloating horizon line. Wind beneath the pits of your arm-bones, inflating that bag of skin. Higher, higher. Without her, you'll be at a standstill, a statue, a rootless tree trunk buried at the torso. Without her, you'll never taste blood metallic, gravel burrowed beneath the gum line, scratching the back of your throat. Backseat an open wound, cigarette burns in places that match inner thigh bruises. Floor model, no upgrades. A choice between color and cruise control. You'll want to be in control. You'll craft scars alongside her body / trophies / igniting nostalgia that burns from the center of your chest, a deep longing for a home / burning longing, homesick, heartsick, heartburn— you'll become her in the days she takes you places no one else can, hours melting into each second, each mile clicking the odometer. Counting time through distance.

You are her: rubber soles heading a banshee's pace. There's no other way to see the world, she whispers to you humbly between gear shifts. You hide machetes in door handles for protection, matchbooks in the glove compartment for emergencies. As the plastic begins to fall off, rot away like a dying thing, you'll eventually let her go. You'll settle down somewhere for good, sell her for $500 cash with an online ad.

Hundreds of thousands of miles down your spine, she'll have taught you how to live.

PACIFIC COAST

Highway 1

The first time: I was three / a family vacation I always pretend to remember (they say memory doesn't start to stick until age six) / I wore a red sweatshirt I picked out with illustrated sea lions on it / my mom said I never took it off / my nephew wears it now (my daughters will, eventually) / his memory and mine are the same / barking animals, endless caves, I swear it started then / I swear the feeling never left my skin

The second time: I drove The Grapevine / slow, then fast in drastic intervals / watched the hills burn to brown / the bay open up like a whale's mouth / I was a plankton / a child lost at sea / not lost, no, I had my sails up— I could ride the wind like I was its master, the whole world mine, not a storm in sight

The third time: I was lost with my dad in Guadalupe / an agricultural community with two stop signs / did we even have a conversation? I don't remember (a precursor to our future relationship, or lack thereof) / we fought about the route, about him wanting to smoke a cigarette in my brand new car (I didn't tell him yet, that by then, I was smoking, too) / I was long accustomed to a car full of nicotine clouds since I was a kid and he'd tell me to stick my head out of the window of his red flatbed truck / I enjoyed telling him no this time, keeping some small part of joy from the man, serving lukewarm dish of karma / I earned a speeding ticket further south, in Cambria / he told me people like us didn't deserve an ocean view

The fourth time: I was drunk as hell / we closed down the bar and I wanted pea soup / there's this place in Buellton, she said. I remembered the sign, the big windmill on the side of the road / I remember the smell of salt licking my skin / we drove all night until the needle marked the gas tank half empty, she said half-full / Anderson's was closed, so we ate gas station soup in the parking lot, watched the sun come up, cried in metronome ballads home / pulled up to our shared apartment— the one with the bay windows and French doors, the one that swallowed the sea air whole and festered it onto ancient hardwood floors / my gas light lit fire-orange-red / this is the night I remember her best

The fifth time: I took a train that stopped every ten miles, it seemed / I debarked in one town, misplaced an ex-boyfriend in the crowd / boarded the next train and returned South / I never apologized, time whirring through big, glass windows over cliffs I longed to jump off of

This time: I had my sights as North as the highway would take me / wet and dreary, I was thirsty, dehydrated, longed for wells of water to form midair / the desert was evaporating my blood from the pores of my forehead, causing my wrinkles, of this I was absolutely convinced / a maternal-line trait I wasn't sure I feared yet (this would resurface at 32 when I chopped bangs across deep caverns of my skin, my daughter wearing that red sweatshirt with the sea lions) / I drove fast and wild, my windows down, cigarette clouds evaporating into tobacco-salt air / I wanted to see the sequoias: the biggest, oldest living thing you can touch with two human hands / I wanted to chew on the bark, swallow the past of the earth, my earth, become some sort of goddess imprinted with the wisdom I couldn't dig deep enough to find in the desert / carving into the earth and sea like it was the only road on earth

DELIRIUM

: a source of madness

: my first love, planted with spinach breath in the after-hours of happy hour martinis, when we acted
  with mature palettes too young to differentiate lies with. An overture of early twenties adulthood;
  something as light as the breeze could sway us in opposing directions. The truth was, I liked its
  body, strong and assuming. Three chugs, and I was weighted into the earth.

: labyrinth assumptions bred from my fascination for Françoise Hardy, classic American
  romanticism that leads me to wear my hair in a scarf on days my insecurities get the best of me.
  Parisian nostalgia and The Golden Age, a psychological disease. I'm committed to the 17th century;
  the Old World. Part of my heritage I'm too nervous to prove isn't true. I wanted to be elsewhere.
  But, so did everyone, in their own way. Former,

: elsewhere. Last call lives between the minutes of this beer and the next. When the lights cast an
  unnerving glow, a time warp sensation that placed me on a different set of cobblestone. Legs
  carried with the muscles of a dropped anchor. Crowds dipped in cardboard, cutouts propped on
  the sidewalk outside of storefronts, like the one of Edward Cullen my roommate carried in her
  trunk for two years— we were too old to show it in public. Too cool. Kept him locked in the dark,
  cartoonish, lethargic, pale. Transported from place to place without a single moment of
  acknowledgement. We could be on Mars, and no one would bother asking for oxygen. Disdain
  translucent, my skin, translucent, pink junctions deepening

into magenta, swallowing me up. I sat at
 a mosaic table meant for two. Brought glass to my lips, miniature and pink. Former,

: elsewhere. Anywhere but here.

33.761397, -118.190282

THE RAINBOW BAR

was propped amongst a western film façade on deserted movie lot. A backdrop painted

in jagged V's sliced through one-dimensional notes of contrast. The color green appeared unnatural in my eyes; Technicolor so bright it looked as if someone tinted a black and white movie (even black and white films are made up of shades of gray). I couldn't find the sun if I borrowed it from beneath my follicles, chemical stain seeped into my scalp. Natural was a lost cause. Nine p.m. on the dot: the world remained a faded version of daylight. It was as if the curvature of the earth stretched time around a globe and chose high noon forever. The Wild West, Montana country. I couldn't spot a single car, but heard a highway of traffic— later, I learned,

a river. I'd do this often, mix up sounds and smells, unsure if I was dropped on an unknown planet or floating in the middle of the sea— I might as well have been. Water now running instead of pushing and pulling, sky sitting still instead of breezing and blowing, through wooden windows and cotton curtains, I thought damn— I want a big fat ice cream cone in my hand and a derringer pistol strapped to my thigh at a time like this. I had forgotten my hat, blue-brimmed like Montana sky. My blisters filled with blood with every step I made in those department store boots that would never become worn-in. The sign above the saloon was hand-painted by a third-grader in white-out, or so it appeared. Heavy door fashioned with iron-fisted oblong door handles. And my mediocre grip that I just knew everyone was going to call me out on.

46.24767, -114.15758

IN THE NEED FOR GAS MONEY

A back room full of Wisconsin blondes, a reflective moment, a notion of resilience. I could smell the specific age of asphalt from over six-hundred miles away. A rush of adrenaline: a runner's high.

There had been cuts in the inside of my palms for weeks. I snipped more cotton from the bottom than the top and let too many men define my strength. The truth was, I missed the salt of the ocean, the frightening possibility of being pulled out into space, the obsolete-chance-yet-still-possibility of washing ashore on a deserted island to die in paradise. In wild contrast, a freezing lake: floating bodies and plastic synonymous. At the bottom: wrecked in search of the sea, my limbs blue and bloated.

When you think about it, it's always the money that makes an act scandalous— best and worst intentions displayed like chunks of meat sold at market. In the distance, train tracks rattled the moccasins that still make my feet sweat and smell in embarrassing ways. After so many years, I've hand-sewn the soles back through the trail-softened leather. A yawn in the audience, the hundred-dollar bill crisp in my hands when it was all said and done. A definitive. Reward at the lips, the gums, pennies under the tongue.

I never minded the yellowed tinge of gasoline spilled on my knuckles after a long drive. In fact,
I welcomed it.

39.0676092, -108.5652862

CARNIVOROUS SKY

Imprinted:
cannibal crows
sliced watercolor palettes into two divides:
the city skyline and
the rising Monument:
the Western Slope

This is your view from the top of a ferris wheel, three beers and four shots after the suggestion of a bartender in warm flannel lightly took your wrist and folded red paper tickets into your hand.

He left paper cuts in places that will take long to heal, but that doesn't matter just yet.

SNOOK'S BOTTOM

is a watering hole one dirt parking lot from the Colorado River. It's close enough to the overpass to make the sounds of water and land indistinguishable. An oasis. We crumpled up the last few flakes of mushroom stems and placed them on our back molars, grinding dirt into saliva. Swallowed a mothy, concrete ball. The still water was warm on our skin. Our stolen inflatable rafts— Wal-Mart-thin and weathered from the mid-summer heat— threatened to disintegrate and leave us marooned. But my body was born into triple digits, so this felt like home. The trees began to glitter and glow in the breeze when promised. It became dark beneath me, infested with swimming dragon beasts, and I didn't care. About anything.

Those were the weeks we'd get stoned and watch Forrest Gump under the broken swamp cooler on repeat. Drenched with condensation and the luxury of boredom, we took advantage as house guests in a room with little furniture and too many people. Plagued with hospitality and free hallucinogens, we wandered through cornfields and gullies with expensive cameras, waded through thrift stores coated with dust, counted dimes for happy hour beers in plastic cups.

We floated the raging river like refugees. Outcasts from a society we imagined to have rejected us. Our blood ran wild in our veins, confusing direction and developing electromagnetic fields between us and the center of the Earth. We conjured magic spun in family legend on a dirt porch playing poker and passing joints until the world forgot our own names. Our reputations dissolved in lost memory, us becoming part of the clay, as monuments, as destruction, as the very thing we were always afraid of becoming, but began to embrace without shame. Our skin tied our organs together with a hatred for our fathers until it began to rash and itch from the dry air. Twilight epiphanies laced with misconstrued dignity. We almost hopped a train with four vagrants and a pit bull just to get out of town without saying goodbye.

The rafts popped the moment we got to shore, a mirage on the distant horizon drowning along the banks of the River like a bag of discarded kittens. When the glitter faded, we remembered why our mothers never brought us here. Packed up the Jeep, spun our tires south.

39.149292, -108.749701

PHANTOM LIMB

: a sensation experienced by someone who has had a limb
amputated that the limb is still there.

Limbless, however, is a survivable condition— some more so
than others. I always thought of you as my left hand. A
mirrored shape of my dominant, a devil

on my shoulder. Our blood heavy in our bodies, short
generations from our pumping hearts. I stopped mine years
ago; you restarted ours both. A defibrillator

on the desert border that summer we wanted more, dug
graves under the Monument. You cried when your father died:
a past that I don't remember the same way. I bled myself out

more times than once, I bled my father from my body while
you wanted to fill yourself up with yours, with our Grandfather's
gypsy curse, our family legend, buried as deep seeds in the soles

of our feet. My mother's bones made home in my body instead,
expanding in this bag of my father's blood. You've seemed to
have made peace, remember these men as someone

maybe should. When we found ourselves— each other— we were
understood as same, as
family. Something we both craved with malicious intent to
destroy, to rewrite:

to expand landscapes barren and obsolete, roadways carved
into the lines of our skin
from too much sun. Indulgent as if it were a four-letter word,
embracing the things

we were taught to eradicate. My phantom limb, my hand I cut
off to bleed myself out, before

I knew better. Charred flesh at the wrist, you exist not in pain, but

: sensation. We are a part of one another, and when life becomes impossible, when others do not understand how to read the road

as a living goddess, as a part of our bodies, as our historic pasts, as heritage conflicted and coarse, this sensation pulses and the wind howls,

and I remember you whole.

I KNOW I SHOULDN'T

but that liquor trigger's dripping in the back of my throat like distorted guitar riffs in an underground brickyard where everything smells like worn denim. I wonder how much more metallic the E string is from the E string. Pulling beers from a cooler at 4am in a neighborhood I've never heard of, summoned by a group of claim-jumping train-hoppers on a boxcar mission to Alaska with nothing more than a hobo's allowance. Oh— the luxury of freedom, of danger. Goddamn defiance. Anonymity, invisibility. When no one cares I'm dead, disappeared, forgotten— the last fret in a finger picking banjo chord, washed away in sun-bleached decades, folded over in time. How many different sounds come out of the same four instruments? Explain it to me— love in caddy-corners giving the couple by the door splinters as she hobbles up the steps. Nights like these I wish I was that girl, instead.

TEN DOZEN BREWERIES

and a mile high, drowned in stout lungs more suited for sea level. Moisture drunk from chapped lips, the taste of basil, a strong guttural pang that feels like home. Déjà vu. A past life rising like the dead. Maybe it's the downward slope of the bends, rocky peaks once so familiar, now dipping into flat plains east, ocean view of wheat waves inhaled in shallow breaths. Maybe it's all the girls named Hannah whom, when introduced, all remind me of my sister of the same name and how her legs move like my own in muscle memory strides across a room. Maybe it's the way California evaporated from hidden corners of pint glass arches, white-laced and fermented, frothing high in my throat. How I've always imagined mountain air to taste across the chest. Aspens can only grow at a certain altitude, after all. An altitude that kills every other living thing.

Waif-like and fragile, this sensory of home— an inward tug of miles beneath scraped knees, the faraway of the familiar, running dark in rivers I thought I was tired of swimming, like a locket rusted in memory, cold on my hip.

39.760482, -104.982416

LINGER

is deceptively swanky, coffin-shaped happy hour menus and all. Our waiter is Kevin, well, *Kevyn* as he points out under curly hair pulled back in Levis hanging off his small frame. He's never had the duck wings. *It was once a mortuary*, I'm told, skyline in view like little cardboard cutouts against a paper sky that reminds me of my mother's house in June. I once had a home, but burnt it down with a match during the Santa Ana's one spring. I order a cocktail next to to a rusty green RV carved into the building under a fluorescent sign that reads "Olinger Mortuaries." I can't find the wheels, no matter where I look for them. There's a false originality, evident in glassware that felt too light in the hand, two-toned boat drinks delivered with no straw, a flat world without windows. It's amazing how many places in your life you can describe with the word "flat." Sometimes the sky is blue, and sometimes it is red, but it's never snow-capped in froth fit for a five-dollar artisan cocktail named after pirate Jews in Marrakesh. A sailboat would be better fitting here instead of that RV docked on a rooftop set precariously over an ice cream shop playing Marvin Gaye too loud, crowded with mothers in business jackets and leather-strap heels I'll never afford. I'm uncomfortable in ripped jeans: they're faded at the knees and smell like cats. I've never owned a cat, just a big blue dog I lost in a past life, whose tongue I still dream about on my calves when the world feels too wide for my wingspan. Can you feel it? It's the first day of spring, and all I can think of is how many corpses have rolled over these very bricks.

39.759524, -105.011383

THE OVERLOOK HOTEL

Every room in The Overlook Hotel is playing Kubrick's "The Shining" on a continuous loop on channel forty-two. Once I sink into the white-capped comforter and slip into sleep, I'll never know how much time has passed, just a bottle of vanished red wine to act as timekeeper. Whisky sweats on the backs of my knees lure me into lucid conversation with childhood memory. I've claimed that this has been my favorite movie since I was five— how many lies I've told so many times until I believe them. How many times I couldn't get through the axe scene, triggering a real-life horror show. Why I always sought to be brave. They say this hotel is haunted, but the ghosts I find in closets since I was too small to reach the doorknob are nothing more than companions. But it is my favorite movie, I'll say a million more times so I do believe it, and it some ways, it has become truth.

Not the anticipation of the axe, the blood furling down hallways— it was watching someone's eyes turn a shade of madness, the pending isolation, it was how thin the ice feels under the weight of passion.

Midnight at the legendary bar, velvet-roped in the corner of this grand hotel. Endless shelves of brown and green-necked bottles, sprawled across continents to wet my lips with, to meet the demons settled into all the dark places. Rope lights like Christmas, a familiar scent: pine mixed with second-day alcohol. Blood-letting. That's all this really is. The grandeur of not belonging, the mythic. Like my sister's tarot card readings. Or wearing this nice sweater in hopes of no one spotting the snags under the armpits.

Bourbon, on the rocks. A cheap joke lost in flushed cheeks. I usually drink it neat.

40.383371, -105.519173

SOUTH OF STATELINE

divides Colorado and New Mexico into a disjointed desert landscape that disrupts the horizon line. You've abandoned the sharp silhouettes of the past in a quest for something real to cauterize the tongue, shapeshift that settlement of wanderlust churning in the pits of your joints. There was a word you learned:

Kaukokaipuu

A deep-set craving, carved into the laugh-lines and life-lines from the pores of your face to the fleshy meat at the center of your palms. The fire you feel at the heels of a quickening pace, seductive lure of panic, promiscuity with the road winding on, and on, and on. Sensual abstraction. It cannot be felt as anything else but that: A craving. A panic

for distant lands, foreign soil, by definition: somewhere you've never even been. Sometimes, you don't think there can be a place far enough away. You want to walk there, and that's the caveat. Feet on the earth. Scorched, blistered, marked. Sometimes, you dream of moonscape: barren, endless.

And now, here: Taos, New Mexico.
Barren. Endless.

It isn't your Mojave— desert fruited with green patches and red-stained adobe. A sprawling mountain range, a different world entirely. The longest continuously inhabited human dwelling in North America. Yet— the stars are still violent, the highway still pulsates under a relentless sun. It is home, for now. It makes you miss home. You wonder where home is, today.

You sought to find a hidden hot spring off the side of the highway and failed. Instead, there's a circle of trailers at one corner of the canvas, splayed chunks of raw meat. Across the asphalt sits an adobe building, a sign herding you forward with the promise of a cold beer.

You pop in, pay too much,
sit on a patio facing the *Sangre de Cristo* Mountains,
wonder if the *Pueblo de Taos* considered this
the edge of the world.

36.46476, -105.65983

RATTLESNAKE

warning : a courtesy she does not give. Or maybe, maybe—
she always does. To scare off desert wanderers, make her
existence known, a cautionary hello

Step on me and I'll kill you

spoken as an
        invitation
to die
if
your desire
        to wrestle the edge
        of destiny
overpowers
        her foreboding crow
deep-throated vibration. A rain stick slowly flipped

upside down. I'll hand you a firework and curl into a circle-disc,
I'll watch you light the wick from under a rock. The desert isn't
for people like you:

There are crude signs of warning, anecdotal tales of lovers dead
in sandstorms, from the heat— bodies devoured by packs of
coyotes

I, however, am made for this. Venom sharp
bite waiting:
maybe she doesn't mean to, maybe—

tourist trap / short hike / safety of a ranger's map
red rock horizon / movie backdrop
alone in the bush / run

heed the warning, a siren's wail :
the temptress' shake

WAXAHACHIE

is a dry town, dry as clavicle dust blown in from the highway, rancid with late summer swelter. Oppressive Texas heat sweated me south of Dallas from its Texas-sized pores, annexed, adulterated, with nowhere to drink off of maps folded in wads, shoved into shallow pockets, denim-burns on my knuckles. Sand-scraped kneecaps. A haunted rustle of trees beyond stadium bleachers where football means more to these townspeople than a jock ex-husband does to me, invasive hum of nostalgia from fluorescent lights, tucked neatly in the corners of big Texas sky, fucking *American* sky, where time moved slow enough to stop for some years. I wished

to wade a river, to submerge my ankles into prairie-infested waters, as if I could time travel, as if meadows existed as they do in the movies (they do not). Instead, I picked up breadcrumbs by gingerbread houses on the way through town, off railroad tracks and football fields, over roads of Victorian splendor through rodeo air. I tuned out the buzz of cicadas, foraged and faltered, wondered if I really had an addiction problem because it was Sunday and I hadn't been to church in a decade, because it was Sunday, and in this town, you couldn't buy a beer for at least another twenty-three hours and I was dying to sip suds on the steps of green-stretched pastures. I was dying, I swore I was dying.

Waxahachie: the name of it all. A cow's tail used as a bookmark in the Bible Belt that ran through a reverberating spook in the balls of my feet that ached north.

32.386531, -96.848331

SOUTHWESTERN

winds on the nape of my neck
a passerby / passer-through
change crossing the tracks during a midnight hail storm
a stranger in the night comin' to shake things up
then be on his way

SAN ANTONIO

is sinking alongside a river low, under grey-stone bridges and walkways, gondolas hemorrhaging under the city's water-veins. The whole damn town smells like a dungeon, a faint green cloud that rests in my lungs, makes home in my body, like a childhood memory of an old Disneyland attraction, that specific fetid odor.

Texas doesn't taste anything like the dirt I imagined it would, as wide-stretched as it appears on torn paper maps, nothing like I imagined at all— it's everything wrapped into leather and grown to twice its natural size. Wet. Teenage-hormone-wet. Tourists float by, holding drinks with large umbrellas and I can't find a decent Mexican restaurant to save my life (a problem I'd define my happiness by in later chapters). The city is an odd collection of tropical facade, history etched in Latin culture, tucked behind plaques and flags in motion, Jell-O-humid air. Air and sky that defines the patriotic star differently: ghosts of the Alamo hold hands with heavy-set Caucasians in Texan drawls and souvenir t-shirts: I'm dizzy, grown thick with too many graveyards. The kinds of plots they have to rebury after a rainstorm. Colonized with amnesia. I wander until I find an art district under a mossy freeway, a newly gentrified neighborhood that looks shame-filled and comfortable. Familiar. An aide-memoire of my own dirty history. Dive bar covered in glass bottles, awkwardly caught in a hip outfit on the wrong day of the week, selling Lone Star cans and Texas-sized fries smothered with cheese. I don't want out, I'm tilted, magnetized, and I think how funny it is: how it's always the same bar.

29.425967, -98.486142

SOUVENIR

tank top printed with red, white, and blue
silhouettes of naked women:
a statement piece I bought from a Mexican vendor
on the sand with a bracelet to match, someone else's name
stitched to my wrist. I kissed you goodbye with a slice on my
mouth from the pull tab of a red can. Piss beer

you'd have called it. The blood
tasted like aluminum, you
always tasted like fireworks.
That's how I knew it was time
to leave. I couldn't—

I posed as a tourist on the beach, watched the tide
bring in the bones
of the dead. Shards of sea shells collected by tiny fingers—
I used to do it, too, although something always told me it was
wrong. Like my affection for snakeskin
cowboy boots, and men who
swallowed love
like latex balloons.

32.366101, -117.061755

THE WILD ONE

never aged past 1969. She smelled like leather in the middle of summer. In movies, Los Angeles was always the perfect temperature, made me want to drive a T-top, a phoenix emblazoned on the hood. In reality, I was perpetually freezing, my legs bare to the elements, seasonal depression playing stagnant reels in repetitive cycles. Just by being with her, the whole world could set fire.

A hammer from hell, a soft pack folded over in tight pockets. Chemical-stained scalp. Wrists painted with nicotine and nostalgia. Like the Christmas Eve my dad burned our tree to the ground with our presents underneath it, ash cradling a lone cigarette butt as a talisman (this never happened— a black-box fantasy, false memory, Disneyland snow).

In skin-deep truth, pressing against my organs, between morphed tattoos, I was always afraid of becoming her. Of rouge smeared across yellowed teeth, a few dollars in a tin jar beside an old cash register— the kind that always jams when you hide the big bills underneath the tray. "Day bartender" is code for "over the hill," after all. My internalized destiny, my greatest fear: barefoot and pregnant, lifelong servitude to drunk men in one way or another. Slowly boiling the bathtub until I become my mother. The years behind a bar labeled on painter's tape with a specific expiration date, before the milk goes sour. I gulped down a tepid cocktail, ice cubes devolved into different physical matters. In the wobbles of her knee-bones, I saw a mirrored future and thought: *Fuck, I better get my shit together* for the fortieth time since my hips turned outward and flexed my leg muscles in directions I didn't know existed, flung me to corners of the earth I didn't know existed.

This year's the year, I heard my mother say year after year as she'd clutch a tax refund check like it was a ticket out of town. It was, but there were bills to pay, too. She'll never leave this place, either.

The Wild One didn't give a damn. She didn't have French chateaus bookmarked, photos printed out to remind herself to save for retirement, a final escape route to prove she made it "out." The highways only reached so far, cracked with California sun, like the Martian heat we'll have to grow accustomed to after we've destroyed this Earth. Time, for her, was paralyzed. Freeze-dried. She'll dress in her short shorts forever, serve potato-skinned veterans and that one particular man on a corner stool who's been sipping vodka on ice since 8am. Monday through Friday until the night shift flips over the record and turns time backward to our younger selves. It's then she'll slip on her leather jacket and collect the quarter-tips from those men who drove T-tops down sun-stripped highways, smoked soft pack cigarettes and set the world on fire in 1969.

THE BUM STEER

is tucked in a strip mall parking lot off a country road only a few miles from civilization. Light years. Decades. Enough distance and time hollowed from the living to melt reality when you walk through the door to find yourself here:

Wallpaper hulled like corn, the bar top an almanac. There is no winter here. Damp nicotine burrows itself into the wood, following the grains like a road map. You're driving the car, its erecting street signs as you steer. You can't be sure, but you think you hate it here. A pornographic photograph that you can't stop staring at. Familiar and wretched, it makes you feel dirty. It makes you feel

home, accepted. There are bar flies in the pour spouts, bar flies drinking whiskey out of coffee cups. A stage in the back corner is plastered with posters of someone's idols: their mother's memories. Hank Williams III played here once, the bartender tells you. Her skin is stitched together with basement tattoos and she walks with the bowed knees of a biker. A Harley, in fact, parked right outside, leaned against the liquor store where you picked up eight-dollar smokes. There aren't ashtrays anymore, so the old men are using shot glasses. It isn't legal. Like the powder found in cracks, befallen crystals, caked residue, a quick upper to get you through the dim light peeking through painted windows. It's the high desert sun getting to you; maybe you like it here after all. Maybe you can taste the dust recycled with aluminum rolling into the corners of your mouth like a tumbleweed out back, ashing your lips with paper-cut sized incisions you'll regret later. This place makes you regret

everything. You can't leave— your body parts are selling for bartered goods like a hostage in crisis. What was it called when you fall in love with your captor? Stockholm syndrome. A siege of your pirated morals crawling wounded out the back door. There was no time for sympathy. But with every sip, the notion becomes you. You're painting the scene as you swallow long and hard as if it was your destiny. No longer removed from the photograph.

A skeletal old cowboy with missing teeth sits at the curve of the bar with bottle-bottom glasses and a twitching wrist. His mouth curls upward in a smile that argues with narrowed eyelids. Another old man drinks straight vodka, flirts with the seasoned bartender, calling her *barmaid* while placing greasy coins in the pits of her palms. She was beautiful once. Now, she wears rhinestone bedazzled jean shorts that bulge out her slim thighs into meat casings. Now, she walked with a sly limp and speaks in scratchy grumbles between smoke breaks. Now, she smells of menthols and dirt fields. You miss your mother. You wonder if she's ever seen the ocean.

Night falls and you nurse another cocktail. With the shift change comes several replacement clientele, thirty years younger, enjoying a stiff drink after a long day's work. They are passing through, the same unpaved route every day. Highway litter. The ceiling is dripping with brown liquid— you've stopped noticing the details. Pool balls clunk into one another in the foreground of your ears and a green glow swallows the sound of it. In 4th grade, your math teacher showed a video of Donald Duck playing pool to demonstrate geometric shapes— you tell this story too often in bars. A young man with concrete-stained cheeks buys you a shot. He smells like your brothers would have if they'd gone into the family business and it makes you nauseous. A protective feeling— over this place, the dirty windows, the broken ATM machine. The kitchen with an ex-con fry cook flipping burgers in 100 degrees. An inheritance you were written out of. An epitaph. It's nothing

of yours: the way they all slink silently into the stools like a performance. You've now sat through three matinees. It's been heating up outside since the man with the taco cart parked out front, selling *elote* with sweet chili powder, making you wish you could stay here forever. They're digging up graves, you can smell it. There's a dust storm on the horizon. False guidance that leads you astray.

33.707560, -117.08406

POPS

is an eighty-nine year old man from Portugal who doesn't take any shit.

That's the thing about the old-timers. They'll come in at 4pm, sit in the corner barstool with one knee toward the door, dig a 5 dollar bill from worn pocket, slide it onto the bar, and complain about the stickiness.

Well, if you wouldn't get so drunk and spill that pussy-pink wine, the damn bar wouldn't always be sticky

another old-timer will gargle in whiskey insults from across the room, freshly-opened sun still glaring off his tortoise shell frames.

Pops will snap his suspenders twice, and lift a middle finger as he waddles up the barstool in seismic shakes. He'll adjust his leather belt and spin the corners of his mouth deep, deep south.

Fuck you, you mudda fucka

and give me a wink. I'll pour his white zin and take his denim-washed bill, keep a buck for myself.

Fuck you, you fucking fucks

he'll gripe. But— if you stay just long enough past the drunken winks to listen between mumbles and murmurs, the hardened bumps on his nose will twitch when you ask him to dance to Frankie Valli and he'll stumble as you lead and you'll ask him if he and his wife used to dance and he'll nod and step on your toes, your hands wrapped through draped skin casing finger bones that once ran waves through the thick black hair of a girl in bare feet in Portugal who loved to drink pink wine.

THE SALTON SEA

The sea itself, man-made, not a sea at all— a lie, a cardboard cutout— walls the scent of dead fish up in triple digits. The kind of heat that sinks into memory, infects the past. Sulfur sun rays reflect shards of bone that make up the sand, stinging aluminum cuts between your toes. You try and remember a time of glory, conjure up specifics, cast a remedy for nostalgia with witchcraft your sister showed you— you ache for lost beauty in the dead. Heroism caught cycling in the bloodstream. Glamorized like a drug addiction swept under the shadows, peeking behind bent blinds. These are ghosts still living. Faces on milk cartons pinned on ruins.

There are dollars on the ceiling of a bar near the welcome sign, one lone cyclist that the bartender warned you about. He's been stealing cigarette butts out of ashtrays; this whole sunken city a pit of ash. Left to rot, floating in the cesspool, a natural cycle turned against humanity like an effigy.

Bombay Beach is more like the name of a war site: saline levels that are too high, the water too shallow. Surface temperatures scolding, hostile. This is what happens to paradise, you think,

in the end. Burned edges left to the sea to take, take, take with a flooded tide, hypocritical and rotted. And when it finally dries up (you've read somewhere) the whole of California will become a permanent dustbowl. You'll cough up enough blood to swim in. It all feels too familiar, too psychedelic. Like an unintentional art installment, abandoned (maybe that's why you're here). You take photos like everyone else, but are the only tourist to get out of their car. Tourist feels like an insult, an arrow through your calves. You can't hear the music over the air conditioning, humming, buzzing, screeching through dead-still air. A soothing reminder that you don't actually belong in a place like this, no matter how hard you've tried.

33.353565, -115.733503

THE OCEAN AND THE I-10

Cacti colonizing
tears that mimic the shape
alongside the highway
phallic, intrusive
welled up, boarded up

like the Hoover Dam. My dad used to make all the dam jokes
he could, every time we visited it (this never got old)

Not like the ocean's roiling waves, manic
and suspect. The sea could never be trusted.

Not like my desert plains stretched out from here to
eternity— I, the only living thing in the world. So many roads
I could take, so many before-s and after-s, pathways
to mythological lands held tightly in different dimensions,
cursed with possibility.

Wanderlust is too romantic: an inability
to keep one's eyes off the horizon line.
Wonder, winder,
wander, and disappointment.

My ribcage has harvested a steering wheel-shaped bruise,
it's fading green into the empty horizon, brown-painted asphalt,
purple creeping over endless red.

Wingspan: endless.
Albatross red. Vulture brown
rotting skins
of snakes and discarded limbs
sounds of sunrise: this the only time I hear it.

From the insides of my car, of my intestines, the gastronomical
tract of the Mojave, traveling, swallowed up, passing through.
Left to rot, digested, thrown up.

Nobody likes it here. We've all come here to die.

when you're at your worst

engraved into a silver flask: my only defense. Brown-fire taste. The kind that burnt the whole forest down. A gift from a lost lover— oh how many of them are there now— I can't remember which one. He knew I liked whisk(e)y, he knew
too many parts of me.

35.473943, -115.449439

DIRTY

woodchips under fingernails and a taste for the hereafter. Like the sound of a cocking gun, impossible to forget the sound.

He walked in strident tongues, with large hands, lifeline cut straight to the wrist. I hadn't known then, but my heartline would soon flay my skin in two.

In biblical times, the sin was removed from the body by cutting it to pieces, discarding the physicality that forced the mind astray. I am Frankenstein's monster—

Lightening strikes against a stagnant sky in seismic patterns.
The floor on fire, corners
of my eyes white. Snowmelt on the edges
of each page,
decayed,

controlled, buried. Resurrected by a voodoo witch. My actions hold no agency,
no soil-drenched soul of my own
to mourn.

IT COULD BE ANYWHERE

but you're here, swaying to the beat of Stevie's tambourine

you'll know, and you'll know

in sheer-kissed fabric against ankles powdered dry with the dust of a lost road.

A silo town behind a dilapidated convenience store, the color green left behind in the 50's.

Almost out of gas in a forest of wheat plains, hills that rolled your soul like a steamroller

flat until the tar dried thick on the skin. Close your eyes, breathe it in. They call it the dust

bowl for a reason. Dollar domestic on wet lips craving the answer for a familiar voice

on the back of your hand. Too late, barn burner. This fire sky's been following you

everywhere.

IN THE DEEP SOUTH

Bugs as loud as car alarms, sweet peach skin assailants on a late summer afternoon. Hurricane squalls off an Atlantic coast brought in sea birds rudderless against a building of antique bricks, yielding no survivors. The dead unburied, left witness to rot and rebirth, sprout wings. Cobblestone meanders under low-hanging branches displaying robust spines for trunks, fingers along bark highways, invisible webs. We're stuck here now, ankle-deep in soft soil. A stranger down muddy alleyways leads us through bayou banjo plucks, a swamp-colored porch, a backwoods-rigged watering hole where the only alligators around are stretched across steel-tip toes and around slender blades on the hips of locals casting suspecting eyes to new meat. City-fresh, clean arches of feet. Cartoonish, dark air loiters through drooping mist, velvet curtains with the ropes tied to the side, painting over the sun with heavy-bodied oil paints. Over-pigmented blues and greens. Biblical, ominous. We smell like winter snow, rotting in an ice box and molded over on the long drive. Our bodies are cluttered against taxidermy walls, carcasses filled with cotton. We match the bar flies shot for shot with empty stomachs to prove our worth. A still-life moment to remind the rambling mind how heavy time moves in unfamiliar air.

29.928790, -90.085372

PANAMA CITY BEACH

where I slipped my denim cut-offs from one leg and lay on my chest, felt the needles cleanse my bare skin for the first time. I was saddled between past and present: my skin would look foreign in future photographs, virgin, clean. Un-dirtied.

A stranger's hand rested on the part of my thigh I can never hit right with a razor, stinging gooseflesh around my ankles. I wondered how ashamed my father would be. Distance carried me here, not rebellion, I knew. He wouldn't believe you if you tried to explain. I had only been drunk a handful of times before I left home, but I smoked an entire pack of cigarettes on the porch my father built just to spite him. Left the smashed butts in a fire-ant pile pyramid. There was no bandwagon to board, no restitute sense of dignity to cling tightly to. I wondered what spirit had infected the soft pads of my feet. Caused this consistent sensation of pins and needles that kept me on the run.

When the artist was finished, he wrapped my hips in cellophane and handed me a small tube of ointment. The red of the rainbow was crooked, I noticed. I said nothing. Instead, I swam in the ocean right after, even though I wasn't supposed to, trying to bend the red beam straighter, more direct. I read an article once of a man who died of botulism from swimming in the ocean afterward; it's considered an open wound, after all. These weren't Mexican waters, but I could see the wall from here, across the gulf, the jellyfish water stinging my body in electric patterns. I fished for tentacles with my fingertips but couldn't reach them. It was only the sea. Waning, warning, calling me through Morse code, our cycles in stride, tidal, without roadmap. An open wound, I thought, collapsing into shock waves.

30.176591, -85.805488

SAND / CEMENT / GRAVEL / WATER

: a verb, as in
>to boat, to travel, to go
: a metaphor, as in
>a wooden hull, splintered at the seams, fording calm waters.
>Waters we've sought out for their tranquil passage, for the easy route. This vessel, my body: two parts sand, one part cement, crushed gravel, water—

I was eighteen when I forgot how to swim completely. I flailed like a drowning dog, cement blocks casing my feet, poison liquid in my airways. It was as if the drain at the bottom of the concrete basin of the community pool would suck me through to oblivion, to another side in black-hole chaos, my skin ripping from muscles and tendons, snapping like sci-fi movies set in deep space, somewhere we'll never understand, no matter how much our bodies are made of stardust. I was made of much less: water-logged and prune-fingered, I sunk to the bottom of the sea.

I later learned that I did not forget how to swim at all. My body simply refused to counter-balance the element of water. It became water. No longer a sac to fill, I was emptied out and melted into the waves, lost to the rhythm of waning tides, by body part of the sea itself, untethered to land.

In truth, I never sought the difficulty of treacherous waters, of unsafe voyage. I liked the sea calm, my body easy to navigate. I never saw beyond the other shore, even still, masquerading as a wanderer, set off to find adventure in distant places built for heroines and cartographers—

I remained still, crashing waves at the tips of my thighs but no higher, the panic at bay, the chaos powdered into a paste within my bones.

They all thought I named the stars with a fearless fervor— a universe held tightly between oceans. But, I was easy: boating cautiously along a familiar shore on a quiet night, always. My body filled with sand.

KEY WEST

Hemingway linen decorates ocean-blue skies, clouds misted through layers of azure, salt in my nostrils that burn in rings with deep breaths. The air is not as heavy as I expected— it breezes over my skin full-stop, hands around a sticky margarita in a plastic cup, Cuban-colored stucco on each block. Some of the cats have five toes. I had a lover once who told me he did, too, just like Hemingway's cats in Key West, and I believed him. As with many lessons, this was one in naivety.

As is the ease of sailing: I bobbed in the middle of the ocean with a life vest on and vomit in my throat, panic slow-growing, nefarious, like fingernails after death, an entire universe lapping at my toes. The streets of the city filled themselves with wedding parties, bachelor parties, over the hill parties, and I stood swaying in that pinkish, end-of-the-day sunshine that felt like the temperature of something ending. At the corner of a street where a house lived, hidden completely by giant palm leaves, I wished I had belonged.

24.551204, -81.800615

TAMPA

Streetlights hung with thick cables, city-parts
swaying with high winds in spontaneous dance, hurricane-
blue salt at the tips, hair crusted with
mint mojito sugar water, sweet tracks
laid over diamond-sharp sand, calm gulf waters

It's the only place you've seen streets like these:
white sand whipping freely, reclaiming asphalt
with shards of seashells, ground finely into some
version of dirt that somehow doesn't turn to mud
in the rain

This bothers you—
Wet sand cemented between bare
toes. Palm trees howling—
These aren't your Santa Ana's

26.131581, -81.807443

CHARLESTON, SOUTH CAROLINA

bled memories down the skin of my inner thighs in places I hadn't let a soul touch yet at that age. In more ways than one, nightmare façades and distorted figures were whitewashing history wearing khaki shorts. I loathed the inefficiency of the cargo pocket— I wanted to crawl inside of one and light it on fire from the inside out.

Lucid: the Before

Seventeen: thrashing in Jello-shots and mutiny, sipping a sugary-sweet liquor beverage I'd never like to admit to drinking. We held the necks of them tightly. Protected ourselves from the lurking dangers of frat boys, from their inability to swallow the truths of someone else's autonomy, of a girl's right to exist, of their own privilege to, beyond their trust fund prisons, outside of that suffocating pocket buttoned loosely against their legs.

It had been well over a decade since I watched her disappear into that dark room, her feet stumbling between memories I hoped she's forgotten— I wish I had forgotten, I wished they had failed me, too. I still have the hotel-sized cheese grater I stole at that party, rusted and bent, like the cannons at the Battery we'd straddle and talk until we'd lie to ourselves and say that we had forgotten it all.

Not today, I thought: the After

Since then, the statues began to burn down, but they've sewn extra buttons onto their pockets as a result. Wear their pants tighter. To hold on to a history we never agreed to broadcast wildly. It's a lost paradise, now, the buildings boarded up for the season, sleet on every wooden sign, causing an atrophy of the coastline. Fleeing in masses, the sand of the eastern shoreline, stolen trophies, a distant memory.

32.982183, -80.070655

JACK OF THE WOOD

The stage caught fire: I saw this in a dream. The whole wood ablaze, the present engulfed in gasps of oxygen. A widow's heart attack— they all died days later without a single burn on the skin. The things that make a tooth go rotten, infect the whole mouth.

RECORD STORE DAY

I thumbed down a narrow street in a seaside town, each storefront a different page to read. In the crisp, over-read bottom of one, I skimmed crates of old cardboard until I unearthed it: my first. It had been calling my name since before the day I was born. New skin shedding to reveal something very old.

This was how it began: a growing collection of poorly preserved vinyl records, albums that would shape and define the life I found when my bare feet met hot asphalt. A deep-rooted nostalgia, my drug of choice, unkempt contagion. *Always a different obsession with you*, my mom would tell me as a child, right before it'd stale and stagnate.

I've thrown out all the plastic sleeves of mine; they were harder to carry in my arms that way as I moved from place to place. Warped and disfigured, the covers ripped and waterlogged, my keepsakes are not worth any money. Instead, they tell stories of hands that touched them: hoarded grooves are filled with human skin, with stardust, each melody a christening moment. Hands that played the same songs for decades in a different world, one that hung in some sort of balance, before.

Physical manifestations, sought to die and melt in the apocalypse, as mortal as you and I. The illusion of immortality, the loss of time it takes to get up and flip the record over, so many things that can happen between seconds.

Record Store Day is not for people like me, people who hold no value in the "value" of their vinyl collections, built for show and prestige. I don't apologize for this. I'll keep listening to that tinny scratch over a fuzzy speaker, adjust the needle over Grace Slick's voice at second :36 each time. It's the past, the before, the way that after all this time, we've survived in different bodies.

THE CENTER OF THE WORLD

I was prepared for dreamscapes vast and vertical
Me: a tiny dot in a crimson universe, black
hole, dying star-parts fleeing their space in
space, eternal, visceral—
landing on a planet I was born to, after all this time
feeling alien.

I was a small fish to fry, in the big,
bad city. The center of the world:

It was the heartbreak of my life. Like
meeting a lover after years of distant
communication
by letter, by post, by carrier pigeon, perfumed
pages wafting every step until the day you
finally touch skin. The day you realize she's not

the one: glittered thighbones collapsed under the weight
of catastrophe. Towers shatter, disappear in view. A gaping
hole. Why?
How could this happen?

I was destined for this place, I
thought
I'd be done running, I
thought
my toes would curl into the concrete in an
embrace. I thought
I found someone that I truly loved, but she
was not my person: a

dreamy façade. A back lot one-night
stand we took too far.
A memory that never took place.

36.102371, -115.174556

NEW JERSEY

New Jersey— it's is a dirty word, isn't it? I asked him with genuine caution. When I was young, New York was the center of the world, of the universe, of everything. I was taught this in history books, in the falsified way sunshine curved and sought refuge between structures in movies, low light, quixotic. Tall buildings physically scraping the sky, shaving inches from the atmosphere, minding the gap between you and infinite space. It was some sort of Mecca—

after all, nothing interesting happens in New Jersey, he answered. Reflective moments hinged on stained porcelain mugs, routinely filled by a walking apron. The waitress' orthopedic wedges stomped linoleum as if she just woke up here one day without a reason to ever leave. The coffee was cold, the air was colder. Colder than I expected, colder than Carrie Bradshaw had me believe when she convinced me to wear stilettos on frozen sidewalks my first time. I rode the bus in, and I took the bus out, a bruised ass and a new friend chaperoning me across the bridge, across statelessness, as if I'd never hit the turnpike alone.

I hadn't, not yet. The grease from the griddle sat in the creases behind his dimples, guiding jawlines to sharp places I was sure to get lost in. Nobody escapes Jersey, I said, stirring until I'd turn water into wine, the waitress in my hindsight, my foresight, the spoon hitting the sides of my heavy-bottomed mug— the kind you can only find in roadside diners— a turntable of repeating sound, the needle digging into the small of my back. My mother was a waitress; I was too, I added.

An expression more forlorn than intended, a whispering thought misplaced in my inability to keep some things to myself. It was my biggest fear,

truth be told. A running caveat driving that seven-generational curse,
    a running reason to run and run and run, the apron a heavy weight of chain,

     the linoleum floor smelling of seraphim, of
formaldehyde, my entire life
     dependent on whether or not I stayed in that
diner one moment too long.

40.750610, -74.163918

AMERICANA

boiled and blue: an ebb and flow of memory, failed and imagined

teeth blood-stained, a fire-breached
flag turned black, sandlot-smell and leather

tinged fingertips. You don't like hot
dogs, bicycle seats, or fireworks. You

long for a real parade but can't bear to stand for too long. A
callous representation: how everything looks shiny in
retrospect

privileges that dictate that tiding memory,
loss of self. Some people's grandparents actually weren't
that happy in the '50s, you remember this—

Your grandma was married at 15, in victory curls, while novel
manuscripts rotted behind couture housework, behind a fantasy
of travel. She had many ideas of what you were "to become" : a
writer, a world-changer, a mother

suffocated by an idea: chasing Americana
with cult-like obsession, retro-

vintage chloroform, yellowing and warping the edges of every
photo until kids start to think that's what things actually
looked like.

41.681759, -71.561267

OHIO

has me singing Neil Young, dust in the lungs, commitment on a highway I only knew the verses of

I drive under a bridge weighted down with overgrown moss and I might as well be driving across the surface of the moon during the brightest day on Earth

> / My check engine light sparkles red, but I haven't began to worry yet

There will always be a tinge of rejection in my mouth, like metal, like tin foil against a once decayed tooth's filling— even porcelain teeth are hard illusions

> / I haven't heard from my best friend in almost a week, and when I finally asked her if she's ok she responds: *better than ever*

Our cells began to die even after we learned to check our privileges before entering certain conversations. It's why people are always more comfortable in smaller circles, where their white knees can touch each other's, voices echoing ideas like parrots validating the wrong color of the sky

> / Death is simply a series of smaller deaths

It wasn't a simpler time, no, but I still wear my hair long and unruly, a faded camouflage jacket tied to narrow hips

LOU ELLA

I'll sit with her for a while, watch ice become part of a different matter, us becoming less ourselves, and more like our counterparts. The ones we order everyplace we go, from dive bars to cantinas to champagne brunches. Lou Ella's been ordering gin with two rocks since she was fourteen— her brother's idea to make her sound older than she was; it worked, her mouth smelled like artificial pine trees since the day a locomotive split her daddy's car in two, since the day the doctor scraped her womb clean with objects she only felt the shapes of, since Papa Lou felt the toe of her rhinestone studded boots one too many times in the head until there was no one left but herself.

There were certain things you lived with, and certain things you lived without.

IT'S JAZZ NIGHT

at the Meadowlark, cool saxophone opening a vein measured by decades. I read once that our pretensions are all we are. Exposed bricks, mortar crumbles beneath fingernails. I've already spilled Fernet Branca on my white shoes and it might be a sign. I've been tail-chasing drum kick heartbeats since I was a child, music like fresh air built into six-cylinder streams. Kansas City underground felt like fiberglass, the way the basement echoed with saxophone licks, like hunting wild onions during the prohibition. Midwestern mud in prisms on palms, my fingers could never move that fast. Mystery held in cheeks, revealed in a series of notes that for some reason make sense. Or do they? There are two men discussing the math of it all. Under black-rimmed glasses and a trumpet pulse:

— *you swing like a rusty gate*
— *you can't swing a bag of shit*

But I can swing from my hips, and with the electrical-tape smell of a baseball bat handle, and on the backs of strangers I swing a high and pure as the playground in July. My knees are swinging in my steps.

39.035167, -94.567001

70-W

This was where I was created: the middle of Kansas. A moment of conception. From the point on the map, it appears everything was conceived, created, blossomed outward, from middle to end. River veins flooding life into endless prairies, before men took harsh lines to a map to carve out shapes of states. A perfect little rectangle containing a mass of open space.

That's what I am inside: simple, desolate, open. Contained

on this long stretch of highway, infinite. Like the sea, like the desert, this same horizon blurs over landscape, endless. Fields reach for miles, farther than my albatross arms span, regardless of dismissed speed limits. Dirt roads that lead to places I'll never find on this highway. The middle of nowhere, the middle of

everywhere. Possibility, a drug, reshaping harsh corners into smooth spheres. New beginnings, new endings. I felt as if I could really run— peel my tired sole off of the gas pedal and actually, physically allow my legs to make a decision on their own. A bullet shot into the sky, gaining speed in its descent. Strong

legs, like my sisters', we could snap a neck in half. Legs that deserve naked kneecaps under virgin, Midwestern sun. Simplicity. Boiled down, sanitized. An affinity for a time that never was, a bleached experience, white-out across pages that darken my edges. I had very specific, reoccurring dreams

as a child: I lived on a farm. This was long before I understood much of anything, before I stopped consuming the dead, before I realized the whole world smells like shit. But, in my mind, a farm was
this: sun

flowers, open fields, blossoming meadows, late afternoon sunshine. Small groups of animals that served no purpose but to add to the aesthetic. Chirping, rustling, easy-peaceful sounds. On the spectrum of my waking life, my actual

childhood: hard, loud, alcohol sounds. Slamming doors, broken kitchen appliances, police sirens. Here in Kansas,

it smelled exactly as it did in my dream: I was a huge bird, demanding space in the sky, circling overhead, observing, circular objects, coded. Red silo, green grass, yellow tractor. Simple, easy, peaceful. Dorothy slippers, a tornado on the edge of the earth, destroying everything in order to devour my body. A low rumble, I ran through a cornfield on the side of the road for the first time in my life. I returned with cuts down the sides of my arms, bleeding.

It was the middle of the night when I stopped this time. I'd been here before, this particular rest stop. Low hum of idling semis rumbling the pavement under me. Legs swaying, landsick. Miles between humanity. Pupils wide with road exhaustion, I could drive it blind. I-70 was a pathway from one limb to the other— I knew it like my own body. But tonight, I was a stranger. Hoards of buzzing insects clouded the building, the parking lot, vanishing point.

Biblical, blinding, assuming. An eerie green glow, hovering in the thick, midnight air. A tornado warning hovering between lines. Hanging loosely onto the fabric of my clothing, tugging gently— desperately— begging me, downward. Into the wet earth. Truly, a serial killer

scene: one light busted out above the restroom, a humming breeze whistling through the grass blades one by one, whispering my fate like a game of telephone. Hairs stood stuck as needles across my skin; my sunflower's petals fell one by one as I swallowed a cicada whole. Choked on the rolling hills. Re-birthed

my blossoming existence, re-created as a living thing, an evolving creature, the world inside me flat as the map of Kansas.

38.87861 -99.18461

OFF HIGHWAY 55

there's a bar in the plains named after a man with a mustache and a gambling problem several miles south: Doc Holliday's portrait doesn't belong in these oceanic wheat plains, surely not this menu, but I ordered a grilled cheese sandwich anyway. We had been driving since Minneapolis and the cloud cover low on our axles tinged a thirst for a leather-dripped beer and a warm slice of bread halfway to Ellendale, North Dakota. It felt like the first beer of my life and tasted like goodbye. A weight lifted off the backs of our hands. Magnets formed by planets. Air that smelled like tires, the wobble in my kneecaps from driving in a snowstorm begging to settle on safe land. Landsickness brewed in our guts: I never did learn how to sail. It wavered thick on our ankles like tar— a haze drowned by paper maps and a rental car singe that would never be replaced, even a decade later.

We were young then, finding comfort in the way grass blades felt in the cheeks of our mouths.
She threw her diamond ring on the highway and we got drunk off the way her bare fingers felt
in the spring air, where here, it was winter for months after we learned how to spell the word *blizzard*.

45.041907, -93.789133

DAKOTA LANDLOCK

: allies, friends / Dilapidated red pumps that clicked as the numbers scrolled up, falling faded tiles. We filled the car with dinosaur oil and the expectation of forward movement. Sometimes I confused the left and the right, needed my hands to make sense of direction. I'd shape my fingers into L-shapes and bring them up to eye-line, squint, spin a compass and ground the magnet buried in my belly. I never pull up to the gas pumps on the correct side, everything always backwards. Time suspended in overgrown wheat, a hilly highway that rolled like the ocean's tides— one could get just as easily lost, I thought. Left to float untethered to the physics of this world, until the sun peeled back the skin of bones and raptors come to feed on forgotten carcasses. Like dead bodies, we stood there listening to the methodic splat, clunk, chug of the pump feeding gasoline into the bottom of an empty tank. We had driven on zero miles to E for the second time since plummeting off the sides of the earth and into the horizon line, testing fate like a wild game. Like the buffalo on pavement, roaming aimlessly to extinction.

: westward migration / The attendant wore Carhartt coveralls, a hat shading thick glasses. He rubbed a potbelly full of tobacco and liquor with grease-imbedded hands; a suspicious limp revealed hard-earned sympathy that I translated as dishonesty. He nodded in the direction of the bathroom— a simple closet made of PVC pipe and drywall. I nervously opened the dark-lit plastered door, imagined the attendant punching through with his fist, imagined me living right there forever, destined to watch ghost ships pass in the night, child-less swings sway in the Dakota breeze. How slow a '57 Chevy truck would pace at my heels if I ran. Slower than shotgun shells. Than past lives.

: former territory / We drove away with less than a half tank like salmon upstream. Said nothing to one another as we passed under an archway decorated with chipped white paint. A one way road to come, not to go. I realized, passing under a welcome arch spotted with false floral ties, that not one word was exchanged our entire visit between anyone. Phantom words disappeared into stillness, unspoken, all the things we've never said to one another. We never did see a single other inhabitant, save for the limping attendant in coveralls smacking his chew. The entire town, though, reeked of him, buildings saturated with the stench of one lone soul in a deserted land, collecting bargains and coin, bartering with paper language. I knew better than to root the pads of my feet into that cursed soil— I kept my footprints light, a blessing of high arches, nimble bones that bent and shaped under differing barometric pressures. In the sea, I would have drowned.

46.002750, -98.527046

TENNESSEE

was her name, brazen and cool. I knew
it wasn't her real name, nor where she was from—

I knew nothing was real here, dipped in honey tips, forgotten history
in the corners of her grandmother's name. Olive-oil

skin and loose eyes, relaxed in the pockets of her skull. I loved her like a sister, mother, lover, like the best friend I'd never forgive myself for abandoning.

Tennessee's sharp bangs framed facial features they haven't invented
words for yet. In a pink

motel, a window viewed a pink
convertible. It sat precariously against bright blue skies,

Tennessee skies: MLK and Elvis and Dolly and balloons of
violent phantom limbs, thrashing, haunting her skin in tobacco waves.

Her own history a scenic byway: she sat in that chair and breathed me in.
There were stories to be told— I was not one of them.

THE ONE AND ONLY

is the only bar from Mesquite to Cedar City, settled on Main between twenty-dollar motels in a Mormon town two hours north of Sin City. Here the whisky seeps through red clay cracks and evaporates into Utah blue air before it can make it to Kanab, or at least that's what the locals accept. But this isn't a story about locals.

Every few months they come in, fresh glow off flushed faces from neon lights of the Palms motel. Giggling over its sign "Swim Pool," displaying nothing but a cement crater of rain-slick tools and chain link fence. Make plans for summer; February rot still swept under carpets by 11pm. This time her hair is short and blonde— him always the same, unmasked obsession spiraling from his tendrils, never looking at me or anyone else but her. Pitcher of Pabst Blue Ribbon, two glasses, big tip. By now the denim stares of regulars have softened into smiles. *From California to Colorado*, they say. Meet in the middle, calm the nerves with a backpack full of tall cans and rib cages bursting. That's how she looks tonight: bursting. The corners of her lips are tucked back into her teeth, the pores in her forehead open and willing. She can't escape it: 250 miles of road between her and home and it's all across her chest. They'll finish their pitcher, sometimes two, over filler words and finger webs, his long legs a stride around her waist, her laugh catching in his mouth. There hasn't been a love like this: there's cowboys and tourists, desert meth heads and religious fanatics. And two lost lovers, drawn together across dotted borderlines and highway signs, just to meet here.

They say Saint George is the Dixie of Utah. Mild winters, the gateway. Red cliffs and sage scent in the underbrush. I hear the Mojave in her voice, smell the altitude in the way he draws his breath. In a thousand dead towns I'd search for what he hides in her shoulders. It's the only bar for miles, here—

you: a voyeur soul lost in the roads between Vegas and Zion.

37.109156, -113.565734

ZION

There's a place by a red stream I lost
my virginity. Not sexual innocence— but
what I lost, I lost in the same
way:
wobbly legs carrying the torso lighter after-
word, an aching in the pelvis, a pain
that splits rivers wide through the parts
no longer yours to keep
for yourself.

The pure of heart, a sort of salvation
land— a journey that never became
what I intended. Washed dirty,
ever-changed, organs re-shifted and re-
purposed, re-arranged to find homes in darker
corners of my body. At least some
thing could settle, I thought.

A rock
in Southern Utah, my
hill in Jerusalem.

37.188814, -112.998375

SPACE BETWEEN

A million things regrettable, each instance pricking the undersides of my tongue and making it itch like the goat heads that stuck into the palms of childhood, flattened our bike tires, bruised the heels of our feet when we took the trash out early morning before bothering to put on shoes.

The kind of place you spend your life running from, as bones ache and long for air too dry to breathe in. Every room I woke up in from thereafter felt soaking wet.

The ocean once lived in the pits between this mountain and that plateau. The space between thoughts. In a clever ploy to be chased and noticed, it retreated to further corners of the planet, leaving my sandy scape barren and uninviting.

MAN-MADE

There's this secret oasis off the side of the freeway at exit— no, I won't give it away just yet.

I want to keep it for myself, to remember when we fall apart, when all the goats at the petting zoo outside of the gas station bar across the overpass die, too.

36.8932739,-113.9174125

NOMAD

I thought I'd always arrive late, puffing a cigarette like it was my last day on earth. Lines thwarted by orange cones: a detour that directed traffic into figure eight's, circles that crossed hairs in a Venn diagram. It was a hundred degrees and the whole interstate had their elbows hanging out of their windows. Through each tin can, a different song rumbled through static speakers, fading musical notes on the desert breeze, meeting at once somewhere in the future where physics are suspended in an afterlife created for lost lovers, twin notes finely tuned with the dial of a radio not found on many dashboards these days. Lost causes. *Saudade*, melancholy, nostalgia: a genetic disorder winding my veins as deeply as a dusty highway, winding through unclaimed land, preserved and unassuming. An unopened plastic sleeve, a mint-condition still-frame. Desert heart encased in a rusted old beater because I didn't trust plastic— plastic applicators, plastic embedded into cheekbones, plastic guns printed from plastic printers. Plastic cars that melted under the sun and bent with any bother, from a simple caress, the wrong look. My weapon: hands on the steering wheel, her rubber spinning like the barrel of a six-shooter. Protector. Sister. Rebel, rebel, enchanted with the simple idea of running, legless, bodiless. We caught eyes with lovers who sang along, leather seats cracked under a sunroof stuck open. *Wanderthirst*: impermanent dehydration. They prayed for a dry season— we wished for rain.

ZEPHYR

verb : the fear of belonging /
       a soft, gentle breeze
         goddess of the West Wind

DE NOVO

Out of nowhere. Boneless. Octopus limbs. Permeable membrane—soft at the top of the skull. Flu-child: perpetual one-hundred degree temperature, boiled blood, a forehead in need of a gentle back hand, an everlasting fear of the immovable future.

Disruption of routine / of self / of worries on a shelf / the side of the road, next to a carjack during a flat-tire change near Reno / trilling body parts initiating descent / manic wings, rotting feathers / constant movement. Scenery that changes from outside a dirty window. Check the temperature with a hand pressed hard against the glass— roll down the window and taste all the ways that air can in this world. Wonder how they figured out exactly how to whittle the shapes states from earth: map-lines marked as gateways to different dimensions. I always know exactly where I am by the smell of it. Put to sleep by the reflective bumps on the shoulder meant to keep a traveler awake, heart beating alongside the cadence of the road, metronome past, revisited. Bump, bump, bump...

A six-inch blade at the hip. Protection. *A young woman shouldn't travel alone,* they say. Reminded of persistent men, strange men, rapists, pedophiles, always lurking, stealing young women, ripping them into pieces, consuming parts of the body that should remain hidden from view, far from home, from the space reserved for them / linoleum / bubble wrap / lace / womb. No— the road is protection. A familiar body, a mother ground up like coffee and used as compost— crawl beside her, curl your limbs inward, make home in her wretched wild.

Wet asphalt sounds different under spinning tires, loose asphalt, smell of new asphalt, the sensation of new dirt. A rambling open space to devour, full-fisted— all the parts of my body plated in pieces, in servings, in segments. I am a four course meal. A bad Yelp review. An insulting ten-percent tip.

Emphatically so: I am embedded in sound of movement. Dried up with the waters of the Rock-a-Hoola. Abandoned, tides sucked back into the earth, leaving skeletons on the shore and palm trees on the mesa. Called on by the western winds, the eastern winds, the northern winds— I wish to become so light, I'd evaporate and float wherever I was meant to / "meant to" implies fate, something I've rejected the belief of, left to decompose under torn pews and shuddered behind stained glass windows.

My last quarter in the last jukebox that took coin: *Lived in bars...*

/ sung the sun awake and slept roadside / felt the same stickiness shellacked across the bar-top / a million past lives and future selves melted into the same well of dirty ice

35.010991, -115.473355

Previously published as poems and/or flash fiction in other literary journals:

"The Mission Inn" *Fiction Southeast* - flash fiction, 2019
"Pops," "The Bum Steer" *Abstract Magazine* - flash fiction, 2019
"Reflections While Driving on the New Jersey Turnpike" *The Esthetic Apostle* - flash fiction, 2018
"Souvenir," *Soft Cartel* - poetry, 2018
"Lou Ella" *K'in* - poetry, 2018
"World's End," "On the Border" The Cerurove - poetry, 2018
"It's Jazz Night" COUNTERCLOCK - poetry, 2018 (nominated: Best of the Net)
"The One and Only" *Lou Lit Magazine* - flash fiction, 2018
"Linger" *Shark Reef* - poetry, 2017.

Erica Hoffmeister grew up in Southern California, but has been chasing that elusive concept of home since she witnessed the vast, east Texan sky bloom on her very first cross-country road trip at the age of seven. She is the author of the prize-winning chapbook *Roots Grew Wild* (Kingdoms in the Wild, 2019), holds an MFA from Chapman University, and teaches college English. She writes in a variety of genres, from poetry to creative non-fiction, flash and even young adult fiction, and has been published in several journals and magazines. She has received an honorable mention for the Lorian Hemingway Award for Short Fiction (2014), was named a runner-up for the Janet B. McCabe Poetry Prize (2016), and has been nominated for Best of the Net. For now, she resides in Denver with her husband and two young daughters and perpetually misses home – wherever that feels like at the time. You can learn more about her and her work at www.ericahoffmeister.com.